VirginX

poems by

Natalia Treviño

Finishing Line Press
Georgetown, Kentucky

VirginX

ACKNOWLEDGMENTS

The author wishes to acknowledge the editors of the following publications
in which these poems appeared, some in slightly different versions:

BorderSenses: "Our Lady of San Juan del Valle, San Juan de los Lagos,
Depending Which Side of the Border You Believe In" (winner 2015 Poetry
    Contest)
Honoring Women by GAGA (Gentileschi Aegis Gallery Association): "Queen
    of Mexico"
Taos Journal of International Poetry & Art: "Coatlicue and How She Became
    the Virgin"
Voices de la Luna: "Between Wings" and "Virgen de San Juan de Los Lagos:
    Como Te Vistieron"

Publisher: Leah Maines
Editor: Christen Kincaid
Cover Art: J. Michael Walker
Author Photo: Stuart Morris
Cover Design: Elizabeth Maines McCleavy

Printed in the USA on acid-free paper.
Order online: www.finishinglinepress.com
        also available on amazon.com

Author inquiries and mail orders:
Finishing Line Press
P. O. Box 1626
Georgetown, Kentucky 40324
U. S. A.

Table of Contents

for Maria de Dolores, who signed her name X,
for Maria de Socorro, who sang in her sleep,
and for Martha Idalia, mi Mamá

Gratia Plena

LATIN X

for la Natalie Diaz, after "Summary Table of 'X' Derived From Samekh." Mysteries of the Alphabet

We learn *x* represents fish bone
removed from head and tail:

rib cage meant to swim
the full weight of the oldest

bodied creatures so they could
glide, eat, fuck, as if in flight,

Mysteries shows early glyphs
of x as crooked ladder,

vertebrae deprived of muscle,
skin, and fur, deprived of face or scales.

Without teeth, without tongue.
X is ten, a number for digits,

Spot on a map, a bleak signature:
my grandmother's. Her *X*,

a skinned cross turned on its side,
lacking the sheath of letters,

of cursive, those curves
that would allow her to read

the full sadness of her name:
Dolores. Letters without cilia

providing locomotion to the seas
of hurts and light that would come.

I did not recognize my name when Mrs. McAdams spoke to me on the first day of kinder, my birthday. I'd never seen red hair or freckles on a person and was told *no*. I was wrong about how to make the number 2 I'd practiced in Mexico with my father. No starter curl on top or mobius swoop on bottom. *Straight, like this,* she said and made me erase what my father taught me. The treat of the Letter People songs: Mr. M who

boasted in gold how he made all the words of *m*, words I'd never heard like *munch,*
maybe, macaroni. What if he had sung about mamá, mano, miel, molcajete?

My friends say Latinx,
conquer nomenclature,

replace the *a*, the oldest drawing of ox,
encompass *o*, earliest signifier of eye:

O carved into soft stone
to say, *see this here.*

We have Malcolm,
Lady, Generation—

x must have been the first to = MC squared.
Twenty-fourth letter,

this carving of an eaten rib-rack,
had lived to order the direction

of organelles and skin's
taut length, of cuts

of bodies we quarter
and grill, of gills,

of wordless motherless bodies
we cage in cages made of wire x's

at the border, of lungs, holding them in place,
insisting on the melt of soft tissue,

on knife-bone survival.

VIRGEN DE SAN JUAN DE LOS LAGOS: COMO TE VISTIERON

1.
Hundreds of years after you left the body
they dressed you in blue, a clay stiff mantle

lit by a gold weave of stems
curled scorpions' tails

tipped with rose petals
in the middle of a sky.

It is a dress only your mother
could have imagined as she swaddled

you in rough blankets,
as she carried you to water

to tend the grit collected
between your fingers,

in the creases of your palms, as her hands
formed a leaking cup to warm the water

before it touched you because cold made you
cry. How she wanted others to see you if she could

display the threads
of you clearly on a cloth,

if she could sew the pattern that burned
in her chest, illuminate the flood

that nearly burst her ribs
each time she realized your weight

was outside of her body,
when she learned your face was the sole

purpose of her arm, her chest, hands.
How she wanted a cloth

so wide the sky goddess
could see it float above dusty bridges,

stretch into paths where some would pass
too quickly, where promises might not be empty,

where washed hands dripped in blood--
defend you, if needed, with arrows or unearthly swords.

2.
So the woodcutter carved
you as a queen, God's very mother.

He'd seen royal robes
stretch tight at the neck, wide to the ground.

Wanted a summit of blue.
Wanted people to think of sails,

imagine a thick wind
had stretched them into a full skin,

say your dress is ocean,
las alas de la agua,

a sparkling horizon of sea,
a reflection of the constellations,

those that multiplied
in your mother's chest

as she fed you her own beams
of human light.

BETWEEN WINGS

Your arms stretch under the blue garment,
not feathered, not under Guadalupe's drapery of sky,

nor below the hot blanket of holy breath.
Your stiff garment

forms a pair of wings
from the apex of your neck.

Only your clothing reveals
it is you, thin, a spine,

a column under that dress.
The carver left your eyes open,

floated Earth's effigy inside your crown
to remind us of this weight on your head.

It was a retired schoolteacher
who flew the body of an airplane

into your shrine that morning.
Announced he wanted to kill

Catholics, Methodists, and Mexicans.
Crashed between the shrine and school,

between children having lunch
and supplicants at prayer.

The exploding fuselage lodged
in the beam, in the silent spine

of your winged building.
Did not kill

a single person on the ground.

*In October 1970, San Juan, Texas made international headlines when a retired schoolteacher smashed a rented single-engine plane into a schoolhouse and shrine. *The Texas State Historical Association*

COATLICUE, QUEEN OF HEAVEN AND EARTH

1. TRANSIT STATIONS OF THE SANTA MARIA NOVELLA

We met in a taxi when I was a child
visiting Mexico. You, an ornament

in the rearview mirror, strung, swaying,
then stamped to a silent glass candle.

Your face ensconced in relief on gold
pendants draped over the hearts of women.

In white plaster, your silhouette
against my Uelita's wallpaper.

Unlike any mother I knew:
you were a girl.

Point of your nose and curve of your lip
matched those on my ceramic dolls:

fragile faces shelved out of my reach.
I imagined your hands in prayer under your thick robes,

your eyes looking low, seeing the dirt under my feet.
I cannot name the intersections you've created between us here,

what route lead me to this hot train station in Firenze
near this striped marble basilica in your name,

what accident or plan took me a year before—
when all these letters to you began—to land for a night

in Old Montreal, a city named for you,
we discovered, Ville Marie

at the only dog-friendly hotel my friend Jen could find,
planted, we discovered, when circling and lost

by a great chance or gyre,
on the same block as Basilique Notre-Dame.

Inside, I could hardly lift my eyes to the blue-gold
vaulted ocean of you, to the intricate, shimmering devotions to you,

my tearful, miraculous first meeting with you.
And three days later—same road trip—I can barely stand to tell you this—or pray it—

because who believes in miracles now? Who?
But Jen chose—and we were not deliberately on a Holy Mary

Pilgrimage in the Americas Tour—but Jen chose—she told me this *after*—
Jen chose South Bend, Indiana for a one-night stop

on our twenty-hour road trip from Philadelphia to her house in Omaha.
Picked it by finding the midpoint with her finger on a map

before we knew she'd give me this free ride from Quebec
because I asked her if I could see America with her on her way home.

See the heartland and such. Not thirty miles outside of South Bend,
after singing for hours about New York with Alicia Keys,

after driving the blur, of a hangover maybe, that was all of Pennsylvania,
after the rolling green miles sandwiching the dozens of mini-mall rest stops,

after hugging the lip, or was it the tongue of Lake Erie,
after traveling through endless ethanol crop:

deceptive sea of emeralds,
wild-lipped corn stalks in this clearly un-parched country;

this saturated, symmetrical gem of a garden;
this blinding, created, single-hued horizon;

these for-thee-I-sing-to-you-hills;
this for-thee-I-cry, I-cry, I-cry for-you-America, for your hidden people,

shoved through your eyeless mill, your people not visible under God,
your people packing the meat, building the houses, and eating walls of sand.

All of this land I'd hungered to see so beautiful, the leaves waving,
but a living grave, not a fruited plain.

As we grieved, Jen said, *I think*
Notre Dame is in South Bend—Or maybe—

Her face spooked— I do a frantic *this is not possible*
search on my phone and Google confirms

Notre Dame is there
The Basilica of the Sacred Heart here

at the midpoint of our journey.
Our dog-friendly hotel once more directly across from,

a one-minute drive from another Basilica miracle.
Open tomorrow at ten. Fifteen minute parking.

And we ran to the gold dome in the sky,
out of breath, the two of us shaking as the docent allowed us,

since we'd arrived before eleven, behind
the ropes, to see the other side of the grand,

golden silence of the multi-tiered altar;
he mentioned the relic of St. Sebastian, of Marcellus,

paintings I know, stories a good Catholic should know—
and under another sea of vaulted ceilings, blued and starred in gold,

but near the bones of child martyr, St. Severa
and a lock of your hair—to inspire faith with its length,

to inspire faith, to inspire with a pyre,
a sacrifice of saints to speak in unison here; your loss our gain.

And Minneapolis, months later, also in transit,
this time with Dad's old friend Tom Breidle—

after a free breakfast and another free ride—
I had not seen him since I was ten—

he spooned out cauldrons of stories about my dad,
the seventies, their racist boss.

his eyes red-lipped
glossy, tearing up:

We always wanted to defend your dad,
but he always had a comeback:

> *I'm sorry Bolo, I've just always hated Mexicans,*
> *the boss said packing his things, fired after others complained.*
> *It's okay, Harold, your Dad told 'im.*
> *I've always hated fat people.*

and while Tom drove me to the airport, he asked me what I was writing—and—
and months later, ushered this time from an airport, not to, in McAllen,

by poet Amalia Ortiz, another free ride, an offering
I'd not expected: same thing happened with Amalia as with Tom.

They both point out the window, out the driver's side
just as I say, *I'm writing about Mary,* and just like that, in that moment,

months apart, hundreds of miles, hundreds of journeys apart, they both say,
Oh? There. Her Basilica is right there. Want to go in?

There? I say. *Yes,* Tom says. *Yes,* Amalia says. *Yes,* I say.
You, Miracle 3 here, showing off to me, a-glimmer, this constellation

you're creating out of all of these free rides,
intercepting conversations, intersecting them,

building a superhighway between them,
a gleaming iridescent polygon between me

and your stars, your rose window, your rose garden,
your breath of rose, and the rose of your rosario.

She's calling you, Brenda says as Amalia and I huddle under your feet
at Our Lady of San Juan del Valle.

Now in front of this inlaid marble,
facing Alberti's Grecian-style, mandalic temple to you in Florence.

The Santa Maria Novella, my sister, Eileen says—
also giving me a free ride—this time to her house in Italy,

to two weeks to read about you, see about you, write about you.
Tourists hardly go there, she tells me. She's a film-maker, filmed

A Room With a View there, years before all this.
You're gonna die, she says. *Giotto's Crucifix is here,*

Mary's whole life
story on the walls by Ghirlandaio

And it is here, inside, my first day, first minutes in Florence
that I realize the word is too big not to say, not to pray.

I'd only wanted academic, the historical version of you,
the art-for-more-art-of-you because you remind me of someone I lost,

my Uelita. I thought you were the only way to her house now,
not the other way around. The slender chapel walls shimmer here.

Liquid flames dance under years of soot.
I think it is my dead, or my soon-to-be-dead is maybe the why of all this;

there has to be a why I cannot imagine.
Who is dying, I wonder. My tia Licha, my Uelita's sister

because she would like this, votives flickering, their wicks' tiny skirts
swaying under my tears for her, for when I will see her again

in the wake of smoke and that balmy incensed light;
sisters, daughters of Uelita Lola, whose name was X on paper,

all twined together long past death,
swaddled in their daily prayers, with me now

under the timeless force of this plan,
under the weight of this idea of yours,

with me under the nexus of your story in panels here,
illustrated by Michelangelo and his teacher.

I see the fluffed pillows
in the panel of the hour of your death.

When I arrived home from this trip Dad feared,
when I arrived home from all of the trips he feared would kill or divorce me,

from rainstorms he tracked in New Jersey, from terrorist threats
aimed at the Vatican just days before we arrived,

from hurricane Wilma as she formed off the coast of Africa
weeks before me and Becky took the kids to Playa del Carmen.

Don't worry, I'd said. *We'll only be in Rome a few hours,*
as if he knew my trips would be the death of him—

and when I arrived home it happened—
unspeakable—just as the eyeless mill of me

shopped for a box of Root Rescue by L'Oreal,
(means 'the halo'— ha:

see how this is a little embarrassing to
someone who said no to the Catholics?)

That phone rings in my car. My brother
just as I pulled out of the last box store there was—

Mom says dad died. Just like Javi said it.
Impossible. I'd spent the day with my dad,

shown him hundreds of photos, begged him to stay for more—
he was standing, laughing, seeing, eating.

This architecture, I'd said. *This church in Orvieto.*
Look at the scrolls here, Dad.

Put them on a flash drive for me.
I want to see them up close.

I don't know how.
Haven't you read the book I gave you?

No, Dad, I do not have time to read books
on Mac operating systems.

Mom says dad died.
He'd emailed me an hour before this phone call.

I'd emailed back.
Thanks, Dad. Smiley face.

Mom says dad died.
I'd only wanted academic, the historical version of you,

not this you, at-the-hour-of-my-death you.
It was only a book of poems I'd wanted.

A book about your names and quirky miracles
other people believed in.

Darkened with years of smoke and traffic—I cannot un-dim
these moist walls inside of me now.

I cannot restore this fresco. No flash photography
allowed in this sacred room. No seats for the weary in my hollow chest.

No crowd on the polished floor in my excavated ribcage,
this vacant nave, this altar of gone, x-ed out apse of my body.

Only God or an upside down painter
could detect an error on this story board here:

define the infinite blur near the top of this chapel—
ending with the hour of our death.

2. ONCE A LITTLE CATHOLIC IN SAN ANTONIO

I remember what the priest said
the first time I confessed:

You could be a Charlie's Angel
when you grow up.

Me on his knee in the confessional—
I could be perfect one day then,

a sugar cube, an angel,
tall, pretty woman on television.

Armed. Winged. An eight-year-old on his lap,
and he crossed my sins away.

Strange, how your head never bent
to examine me then, how you gazed off camera—

yes, I know you held the globe
and our sorrows on your head.

Perhaps I wasn't
in danger at all that day.

How quantum physicists and artists
prove you with pencils, equations, carbon testing

on your pupils displayed on Juan Diego's mantle
in the ancient city, the primordial hill at Tepeyác,

city of my birth, maybe yours, with infinity
sculpted into the *Pieta*, into perennial loss—

that is where we intersect,
the mark of x.

I lost a father,
you a son.

3. ACROSS ALL BORDERS

How you exist in the nepantla between
those dirty beveled doors

at the Italian transit station
and the ribbed buttresses in Old Montreal?

What we see is but the inside, the cage
of your terrestrial skirts.

It is you who settles in the tragic room
filled with hand-written prayers and petitions in San Juan,

you, a pooled summer lake in Minneapolis, a waterfall
that breathes alive the landscape

of my immaculate
dying.

4. MARIA

Maria: plural of mare,
Latin for seas.

Mar, me mareas.
Dark spots on the moon

were once thought its oceans.
As a girl, marinera, marinera,

I floated en el mar every day,
on a hot, rubbery inner tube,

my mother holding my hand
as the sea stung our eyes,

healed our mosquito-bitten backs,
lifted us like flotsam over white wet lips and cliffs.

If we let go, trusted we'd
not be swallowed,

she'd rush us, our tumbling bodies
powerless to shore.

Seawater, Maria or maria on Earth,
liquid solution, saline in our blood,

nostrils. We buy you in spray bottles at the pharmacy
wash our eyes with you in an emergency

inject you immediately
intravenously at the hospital.

Living water, hearing water,
reacting to words, new scientists say.

You fill Earth's wombs and wounds,
float us in your dark body of bodies,

seal us in thick, smart muscle
when we can breath you into our lungs

before you burst us through the lip
        before you rush us,

                our tumbling bodies
                        powerless to the shore.

If the name Maria is an accident
of etymology,

I am only more mariada.
Babies point to the moon,

say *ma*.

5. DECOLONIZING MARIA

She has toes.
They often resist Earth's rock;

her robes formed from a crush
of lapis lazuli.

        The molten Primordial Mother knew
        to lock a glint of ocean between her ancient, rugged lips

for her own floating couture,
for painters and poets to understand
what to say about her,

so we could ask, then:
        are you a symbol,
        a woman, or both?

Are you a good piece of what is woman
or all the pieces that make women?

        Constructed?
        Constructor?

6. MARY, MOTHER OF THE WORD

Mary Mother of Sorrows, Mary Mother
of Mercy, Queen of Heaven, Guadalupe,
Cause of Our Joy, Our Lady of Peace.

Our Lady of the Lake, Notre Dame,
of Lebanon, Loreto, Lourdes, Nazare,
of the Miraculous Medal Fashioned at Her Request,

Our Lady, Canonized and Crowned, of Perpetual Help,
of Solitude, of Snows, of Confidence.

Our Lady of Fatima, Lucia's Lady, who made the sun dance.

Our Lady of Charity, Gate of Dawn,
Immaculate Conception, Grace,
Good Counsel, Good Help and Good Health.

Of the Rocks of the Pillar, of the Thirty Three
Who Freed Uruguay. Our Lady, Great Lady,
Tonantzin, Queen of Mexico, Virgen de San Juan

del Valle en Tejas, de los Lagos en Mexico,
Virgen Morena, naming your appearances,
too many, over twenty thousand names, I heard, beyond counting.

You are a non-count noun, salt, not granules
diluted miracles en el mar, los mares, the maria,
but the cure to the Living Wound.

Morning Star, the nexus of your names,
self-pollenates—Mystical Rose,
Refuge of Sinners—

like dandelion seeds swaddled
in balmy currents, how they
land with feathery precision.

Life Giving Spring,
Our Lady of Aparecida,
Nuestra Señora de la Asunción,

they contain the whole and the fraction of you,
Virgen of Suyapa de Honduras,
the factors, the multiples of you

across the nations. You, divided
by millions, multiplied
by the unnamed, by those caught

in the mystery of stamen,
in the mantle of semen,
pistils and anthers, those ova

who wait in white
ladles, ovum,
Ave, Maria.

7. MOTHER, EARTH

Seven Flowers,
the Aztecs called her.

Kneeling, me and Becky snapped off
small, fat leaves

from Mrs. Forsythe's succulent ghost
flowers. You know the kind,

gray petals thick as fingers
near pink at the stem.

Her front porch spiraled
in a torrent of green

channels, firm ivies, creeping Charlies,
leggy geraniums; countless leafy

stems, eruptions, cascades
from her painted wrought iron stands.

At six years old, we wanted
to know the secrets of dirt.

Mrs. Forsythe eager—
Just lay the thing face up

on top of the soil like so.
You'll see a itty bitty flower

at this little neck here.
Don't need no buryin'.

Didn't seem right. In the Plant Life unit
we did in Mrs. King's class,

leaves did not spring roots but from seed.
Mrs. Forsythe held a clump of dirt to her face—

Always make sure you sniff it.
Needs to smell right,

her long inhale, a demonstration
of how to smell a smell, *like so.*

We breathed in, learned the flavor
of bagged soil, of dirt.

Took some of her ghost flower leaves
home. Placed their gray, weightless tips face up

on top of the black dirt we dug up in our yards.
Worms came too, into our moms' forgotten pots.

Unsheathed strands, pink hairs
poked out like puppies' thin members

at the end of each leaf she'd snipped and granted us,
unfurled into rosettes, and small fingers

searching for a hold like mine
did en el mar when I reached for my mother.

My own Uelita had a patio garden
en el otro lado, enclosed by an ironwork fence,

draped with azucena and white lily
geranio, rosas, la for de jazmín—hierbabuena, epazote.

She fed us aguacate, romero, jamaica.
Like all of Tonantzin's daughters,

she told Mary pray for us
at the hour of our death.

And her green babies
grew from punctured coffee cans,

burst flames of red lily tongues from plastic
Clorox bottles sliced open,

like Coatlicue, at the neck.
Don't need no buryin'.

8. COATLICUE, PRIMORDIAL MOTHER

In another life, la Virgen wore a skirt made of swarming snakes,
a necklace of small hands and tidy, full hearts.

Named Coatlicue, mother to the stars,
to Coyolxauhqui, the moon goddess.

Was sweeping the temple on top of her mountain
when a feather grazed her; its blazing seed

bored a tunnel into her cosmic womb and formed a new baby god.
The moon and her siblings raged at their pregnant mother.

Called her whore. What goddess, what mother of the moon
could not control the touch of a flowing yellow feather?

Wanted her dead, stormed her as Huitzilopochtli,
the Sungod, born in full battle armor,

and at the moment of his birth, threw his sister's moon-face
into the dark sky for his mother to see;

and at the hour of his birth, watched his mother's face
become a fountain of blood, of twin serpents

writhing out of the warm wound at her neck,
who at the hour of giving birth, created time.

Some experts say the wardrobe is why
they call Coatlicue the original Virgin Mary, Guadalupe:

Red dress, blue robes shimmering in stars.
Feet atop the face of the moon.

Goddesses who lost
their choice and their heads

to set their boys in motion.

QUEEN OF MEXICO
after J Michael Walker's Por Las Tardes Le Gusta Bordar

Don't think of her as anything too special or far away; think of her like a comadre who wants to pass the time playing loteria, wearing soft white tennis shoes on her tired feet, embroidering the bedspread a few afternoons a week. Think of her as you might your own abuela who can and does go for the capirotada, the cigarettes, the long button down bata midsummer. This is the woman who yes may have given birth to Jesus or a thousand boys named Jesús—this is the woman who disregards the borders, not just the big river or el mero mero mar between those original conquerers and this patria here, but los puentes between the living and not living, between the deities, their children and todos nosotros batallando down here—she appears to the people en el cielo, en las nubes, in the rocks, on los pankekes, at the hillside of Tepeyác in the middle of dead winter, unafraid of the desert snakes or the sting of nopales—emissary for that Our Father and His/Their Son. She doesn't mean to make us question their power by popping in and answering prayers like nobody's business, but she wants to make a point. She'll wear a necklace of skulls to do it, a belt made of snakes when it was the thing to do, come in a dress made of stars she gave birth to, and the moon too, to wake us up to ourselves. Wear a crown made of twigs and a blue ball that looks just like Earth, so people could get it once and for all. Doesn't stop crying though. All heart that woman. Asking, never telling us to re-think it all, to have the courage (to take a rose or two) (to eat a peach or two), and obey, please, our mother.

OUR LADY OF SAN JUAN DEL VALLE/ SAN JUAN DE LOS LAGOS, DEPENDING ON WHICH SIDE OF THE BORDER YOU BELIEVE IN

I. INFINITE MIGRANT

I first saw you in my grandmother's prayers.
Daily, she sat up in bed, whispering to your blue-gold

image between her thumb and forefinger.
Her eyes closed. Her prayer

easy as wind passing through the screen.
O Maria Inmaculada. I did not know

you were Mary.
Y siempre
bendita.

And always blessed. Your gown
printed on something smaller than a playing card,

not a wilted melt of blue like Guadalupe's, but two stone-stiff triangles,
each a wing, a sky holding a relief of leaves, covering your neck

down to the moon below your feet. A shape
that would travel well
as a statue–

across the country,
across el Rio Grande. Small

immigrant going north in a pouch
from Michoacán to Jalisco, your body not quite
heavy as a book of prayer

or long as an old man's shoe. Somehow
holy, somehow miraculous.

Dressed in blue phonetics,
a syntax of well-timed

roses, you:
the original migrant miracle worker.

II. MIRACLES OF MISERICORDIA

After my divorce, I finally listened to the words in my grandmother's prayer:
Madre de Misericordia, and I only heard what my English could

unlock: Mother of Miser-something, (Misery?)—
Her back molded into a too soft pillow,

her head under an open window.
This was her routine after she bathed.

Windows open in summer, washed,
her gold strands of hair curled into upside down

question marks along her neck. Her prayer card,
filled with blue, your dress, the waxy card of you

between her fingers thin as
a threaded needle.

I asked her, *why do you pray to this Virgen*
    when it was Guadalupe Mexico loved to burn

        with holy candles, who bloomed roses
        in winter, who I met hanging in the rearview

    mirror of every bus and taxi I'd ever taken.
Porque es muy milagrosa, she said,

Scolding me with
or without thinking

of miracles she'd once wanted:
miracle to end her son's leukemia,

to dry out the pneumonia in her husband's lungs,
for her own legs to stand again, to hold a broom herself again,

and once more sweep dried leaves away, the dust, the dead.

III. MIGRATING LA VIRGEN

O Lady of San Juan de los Lagos,
  your eyes do not look down at us, half-shut.

    It is your dream, the whole Earth you carry above your head
  where we do not fight for land,

and we do not cross one another or jagged borders
    with our own travel-sized miracles: miracle of a bottle of water;

miracle of a photograph tucked under a bra; miracle
  of a sandwich shared, made three million times,

    hundreds of miles away. You want us to swim in the one
  ocean, el mar, maria, your populated effigy,

Great Mother Earth: as the dream, as the dreamer.
  I've crossed the brown Rio Grande,

    three hundred times or more
  with my Green Card, then my Blue Card,

while other children crawled across pale deserts
    hid under helicopters, bridged the two lands

in question with their water bottles and work and bones,
Madre de Misericordia, Mother of Misery, of Mercy.

    The difference between these children and me
    was the color of our papers—

We have papers, my father always said, papers!
  Though I'd asked once if he could tell my mom

    to please dry my back better after my shower
    so the kids would stop it, stop saying it—

    because somehow my back
    stayed wet all day long.

You have the same name as my grandmother's,
  Maria de Socorro, Mother of Mercy

    I am still learning the difference
  between the prayer and the one who prays.

IV. FROM ONE EYE TO THE OTHER

My Grandmother held your image only slightly
  larger than her painted thumbnail,

Whispering *esos tus ojos*
  reflujentes a mi.

She, or maybe it was both of you
  crocheted in the light of most afternoons—

Masses of geometrics, yarns loomed through the hooks your hands,
  constellations of thread to warm our beds,

  to drape over the largest of our human possessions,
our tables, our televisions, our couches, our frightened, cold souls

'Uelita whispering colors of threads into the eyes
  of her needles, *esos tus ojos*

Reflujentes a mi. Now that she is gone, I know she knew the one
  story about the Nahuatl girl,

the sixteenth century church caretaker girl, a sweeper
  in San Juan, Mezquititlan, who watched

the acrobat family practice with their children
  on high strings. Had seen the youngest

daughter fall. Die. Witnesses say, the Nahuatl girl ran to grab you,
  small idol, from the sanctuary.

Made of wood, the juice of orchids, pith of corn and gesso.
  Careful not to break you in her grip.

Her heart thinned to a thread as she ran.
    Gave you to the parents, said, *Pray—to her.*

They did and the girl acrobat came back to life.
    A shrine emerged; pilgrims, thousands

traveled for what could save them and the rest of us:
    to end their night terrors, seal heaving wounds,

disappear the cries of sick or missing children, soothe
    the stiffening limbs of elders, bind split bones,

split minds, split marriages, cure the curse of too many babies,
    too few babies, and too much blood after the baby,

of too little corn, too little rain, too much drinking,
too many bruises after he went drinking,

of not enough money for bread, for shoes,
for not enough virginity in far too many daughters.

Miracles, ofrendas, lilies,
    orange blossoms, the fruit,

what they call your boy,
    sorrowful brown mother,

Virgen Morena, child of their god and our Great Mother,
    Seven Flowers. Mother of His good deeds,

Cihuapilli, Great Lady,
Coatlicue, Tonantzin,

thousands, millions of travelers holding
    thin prayer cards to ask, beg, and give

thanks for your effort to step off
your throne for a bit, Queen of Heaven,

redeemer, cross the border where the grim
stalks of our lives

look nothing
like the blue promise

of heaven—

V. MUY MILAGROSA

Centuries later, my grandmother must have been thirty
something when she heard about the priests
who brought you to Tejas.

The trabajadores
missed you on the other side.
Your intercessions hours, days away

Across a deadly river and possibly no return.
They needed a Virgin de San Juan de los Lagos,
a twin of yours, a facsimile, at least, for their side of the border,

hired an artist in Jalisco to have a replica made,
build you a shrine. Some say their car slid off
the road in the dark mountains in front of the house

where a man and woman fed them,
gave them food, a place to sleep, gasoline,
an offering for the new abbot.

Driving back to give thanks,
the house had gone. This tree. The path.
Tire marks from their slide. No house.

Mexico knew the explanation—
that you'd traveled
as miracles do, without papers.

In her fifties, my grandmother would have heard
    about the airplane and that new Texas shrine.
        How the explosion destroyed the marble, the statuary,

boiled the baptismal font and altar.
And I had asked my grandmother, *why this Virgen*
was pressed between her soft thumb and forefinger

before she did needlework, before the yarns rescued her
each afternoon when it was Guadalupe tattooed
on the biceps of Mexican men and Chicana women,

when it was Guadalupe who glowed in swaths
of warm candle wax in all of the Mexican homes I know
on both sides of the border.

And the room became a prayer
with a woman, a window, and a needle,
Porque es muy milagrosa, she said,

Esos tus ojos reflujentes a mi—
because those, your eyes reflect me
on both sides of the border.

WITNESS

That we make her a compiled human
is understandable.

Sandro Boticelli had Simonetta
Vespucchi—his Venus

for *Birth of Venus,* every blonde
in the *Trials of Moses* displayed

in the Sistine Chapel, the girl,
the one whose eyes beg for a kiss

in the *Temptations of Jesus,*
both Flora, goddess of flowers

for Christ's sake, and the gazing,
camera-hungry flower gatherer in *Primavera.*

Simonetta was crowned grace,
Madonna Magnificat.

Had himself buried at her
married feet when he died.

How else to imagine
divinity than with the faces we love?

It's what we do.

Bear the ephemeral.
Worship what is left.

Mensage de Agradecimiento

With gratitude to all of those named here, for their role in helping create this artifact adding to the testimony of the sacred Virgen Maria Inmaculada, Queen of Mexico and Other Wonderful Places: Rebecca Charo McGlothlin (my childhood friend Becky); Jen Lambert, Amalia Ortiz, Tom Breidle, Eileen Horne, and Mrs. Forsythe (RIP), each of you an essential part of this journey and discovery. Enormous thanks to my incredible, interesting, powerhouse Señor Veggie's Poetry Group: Sharon Womack, Bryce Milligan, Jim LaVilla-Havelin, Naomi Shihab Nye, Eddie Dupuy, Lahab Assef Al-Jundi, Mariana Aitches, Glover Davis, and Roberto Bonazzi. You helped me reign in the gold brocade that was trying to punch out of many of these poems and get to the voices *within* the golden leaf. Gracias for your friendship and for accepting me into your great, warm wing. Many thanks to the warm fabulous staff at Señor Veggie's for their always excellent food and service to us every month. With great thanks to my lifetime mentor and incredible friend, my poet-*sister* Wendy Barker, for her unending patience and friendship toward several drafts of individual poems, her keen eagle eye, and for help envisioning the manuscript as a whole. My deep thanks to my sister-in-law Eileen Horne, for her unearthly model of love and for allowing me time and space at her house in Giove to work on these poems and for day-trips to visit incredible places that were essential to my Maria-Odyssey discoveries. My forever love and thanks to Jen Lambert who brought me across the Canadian-American border for the road trip of a lifetime as part of this sacred journey and with whom I experienced several miracles. I cannot go a day without Jen and my other Polo amigas from UNO for a lifetime of friendship and who often listened to recordings of these poems in their cars as I practiced their sound, so deep thanks as well to fierce and kind Liz Kay, genuine and brave Stephanie Johnson, and wise mother soul, Sarah Mason, all wonderful writers I adore; I love you each! Many thanks to my reliable reader and great (and brilliant) friend, Barbara Griest-Devora who nourishes me at work and at play. My thanks to la reina de corazon, ire'ne lara silva, for reading the manuscript and seeing all of my Spanish words gone wrong and for her generous friendship and blurb. My thanks as well to the incredible Veronica Golos, the beautiful Tepoztlan genius, Devi Laskar, and the wise visionary Sheila Black for their very kind words for these poems. For the incredible boost of validation, I cannot enough thank writing hero, Luis Alberto Urrea for 1) his work and fabulousness and 2) judging the BorderSenses Poetry Award, and choosing "Virgen De San Juan del Valle, San Juan De Los Lagos, Depending on Which Side of the Border You Believe In" as the winner. There aren't words (I tried!) for gratitude to my patient and generous husband, Stewart Horne, who has given me hundreds of hours of space, love, listening, and honest critique, as I created these poems and more to come in what I hope will soon be the full collection. And to my spirit-guide-rapper-son Stuart Morris and to my Uelitas Raquenel, Socorro and Dolores for their inspiration to love and honor la Virgen and her child. And to my own Mamá, Martha, and Papa, Bolo (may he enjoy the journey free now of the worrisome body), without whom I would never have seen.

Born in Mexico, and raised in Tejas between two worlds, **Natalia Treviño** bridges understandings between those separated by arbitrary human borders. She has won several awards for her writing including the San Antonio Artists Literary Award, the Dorothy Sargent Rosenberg Poetry Prize, and the Alfredo Cisneros del Moral award. She is the author of *Lavando La Dirty Laundry* (Mongrel Empire Press, 2014, and finalist for the International Rubery Award and The Writers League of Texas Poetry Award).

Natalia became a naturalized U.S. citizen at the age of fifteen, graduated from UTSA and the University of Nebraska at Omaha's MFA program, and is a professor at Northwest Vista College in San Antonio. Her publications appear in *Mirrors Beneath the Earth* (Curbstone Press), *The Platte Valley Review, Complex Allegiances* and *Shifting Balance Sheets: Women's Stories of Naturalized Citizens* (Wising Up Press), and several journals including *Bordersenses, Borderlands Texas Poetry Review, Sugar House Review, The Taos Journal of Poetry and Art, Western Humanities Review, Southern Poetry Texas Anthology, and Southwestern American Literature,* and is forthcoming in several others.

CPSIA information can be obtained
at www.ICGtesting.com
Printed in the USA
LVHW04s1152250818
587974LV00001B/44/P